Be a Better Boss Handbook:
Every Important Guideline for Better Leadership Skills

JD OBrice

Copyright © 2020 JD OBrice

All rights reserved.

ISBN: 979-8-5741-0630-3

CONTENTS

	Introduction	i
1	Set the Example, and Make it a Good One!	1
2	Listen	3
3	Solve the Problem	5
4	People Will Rise to the Level of Your Expectations	7
5	Whenever Possible, Accommodate Personal Lives	9
6	Be a Lock Box	11
7	Say Something Nice/Kind on a Regular Basis	13
8	Communication is Key	15
9	Fun and Friendly Competition	17
10	Be Supportive, Encouraging, and Honest	19
11	Maintain Clear Expectations	21
12	Regard Employees as People First, Not Numbers	23

13	Reward Any Above-and-Beyond Job Performance	25
14	Make Goals Tangible	27
15	Review Consistently	29
16	Host Social Events	31
17	Acknowledge Milestones	33
18	Maintain a Calm Demeanor	35
19	Admit Mistakes and Never Hesitate to Apologize	37
20	Be Consistent	39
	Important Conclusion!	41

INTRODUCTION

You want to be a better boss, be better respected by your subordinates and superiors alike, and lead a team that happily achieves their goals and then some, but you don't have time to read a textbook and then attempt to apply complicated psychological theories about leadership?

That's why this book is the only one you need. This book is going to teach you about being a successful boss, not about business management or how to complete your own job-related responsibilities. The focus is on the people who report to you: the teams, the individuals, and those mid-level members with subordinates of their own.

At the end of the day, every business is about one thing. No matter your service, product or location, your business is, ultimately, about people. Your customers, clients, and every employee within your organization depend on you to understand this over-arcing principle and to lead in such a fashion that you inspire them all to be the best they can be within the structure of your business model.

This book will teach you how to do just that. Be a better boss. Inspire. Teach others to do so. And all within these few pages of easy-to-follow instructions, principles, and occasional nuggets of wisdom.

This is a handbook, not a textbook. Pared down to the most essential points and why to implement them.

Read on, and welcome to the right side of leadership.

Be a Better Boss!

1

Set the Example, and Make it a Good One!

This is really an extrapolation of the Golden Rule, which states, basically, to treat others the way you would like to be treated.

In setting the example, practice the habits you would like your employees to practice.

- *Come in early*, even if only by a few minutes. An added benefit is you'll be able to get in a bit of extra work.
- *Greet each person with a smile.* Want a better work morale? Start by setting the mood yourself and let the general culture be one of pleasantry - a place where each employee feels welcomed.
- *Let your comments about others always be positive.* Or at the very least, not negative. Very often the source of drama and a negative work environment begins at the top. Instead, be the source for a calm and positive work environment.

You are certainly aware that a management's own work culture sets the tone for the entire organization. Each one of us has, as some point, worked in a place that was uncomfortable, if not downright awful, and all fingers could legitimately point to the boss. Remember, you set the tone. You set the example.

You are the Boss. Your employees will learn from you and FOLLOW YOUR EXAMPLE.

BE A BETTER BOSS HANDBOOK

2

Listen

Listening is an important people skill that is useful in every facet, but especially in the boss-arena. Many of your employees will have come from a previous job where they were talked "at," talked "down to," and whose opinions or concerns were readily dismissed.

Resist the urge to react to what your employee is saying until it is clear they have said what they came to say.

In fact, don't react. *Respond*.

There is a distinct difference. If you make the choice to react, then you are being defensive to some greater or lesser degree, which, in turn, sets the tone for the rest of the conversation and will likely put a kink into the flow of communication or cause your employee to clam up because he/she has realized you're not really going to listen or you don't care about his/her point.

When you choose to *respond*, you are changing the tone of the conversation from a fencing match to a game of catch. You pay attention, and then speak, responding to your employee's discourse because you have *listened* to it.

While this certainly doesn't mean you are going to agree with every point or grant every request, the fact that you listened before taking up your side of the exchange will work to your advantage in a specific way: your employees won't be afraid to come to you. Let's face it, while many bosses claim to have an "open door policy", most employees know better and have a sense of dread when they know their job will lead them through that door and into a conversation with you.

Let them know it is a safe space, and that even if their request or concern is turned down, there was no fear in the process.

Pay attention. Listen.

3

Solve the Problem

Grousing and second-guessing makes everyone uncomfortable.

When a team member comes to you and confesses to a mistake or brings a problem to your attention, your FIRST response in the matter should be to *solve the problem.*

There is no need to wring your hands, raise your voice, and prove to one and all that you are the scary beast they always knew you were and everyone really *should* be afraid of bringing anything to your attention.

This - solving the problem - is one of the absolute most powerful components of being a supportive and encouraging boss.

Of course, there will be times you have to correct/discipline an employee, especially if the error is a frequent slipup or the fallout of the mistake is particularly costly. But, even so, correction comes *after* you solve the problem.

When your employees see you first pouring your energies into solving the problem, you are also setting the example that the customer/business matters are the first and that correction will be done after solutions are in place. It will encourage the sort of creative thought in each team member that will result in proactive processes - the sort of habits that may circumvent the problem in the future.

And all because you solved the problem. First.

4

People Will Rise to the Level of Your Expectations

Of course, there are some exceptions, but by and large, this concept holds true.

When employees feel put upon, judged, or sense that management (you, the boss!) is silently or audibly accusing team members of cheating and stealing, the incidences of such infractions will manifest. And that's not just a "manifest" philosophy.

When the boss is encouraging, when the boss tells a team member that he is well able, that management is excited to give him/her a new responsibility or challenge, or even that the company is pleased to place such trust in that employee, the results are nearly always positive.

In short: expect stealing? Looking for all the ways employees cheat the company and steal from it (whether office supplies, time, productivity, actual inventory or ideas)? That sense of distrust will be palpable. It will slip out in conversation in a myriad of ways, and that dishonesty in your employees is exactly what you will reap.

Ever heard the term "you reap what you sow"? It's true. And it's a valid comment for this point. You plant trust and encouragement, you will (again, with a few exceptions) reap trustworth and well-able team members.

Try it. It's the method used by the best managers in the world.

5

Whenever Possible, Accommodate Personal Lives

You have birthdays, anniversaries, celebrations and special holidays in your life.

So do your employees.

Their kids have recitals, school plays and sports, and their partners and spouses have their own events which they are expected to attend. School schedules. Special projects. All of these things and more are very important to the personal life of each team member, and the ability to attend and be fully present at such personal-life-enhancing events is essential to an employee's feeling appreciated and having a real sense of work/life balance.

One of the most common complaints from employees is that their company lacks any respect for work/life balance. Well, Boss, you have the power to give them that sense of balance and in so doing glean respect and appreciation.

It's a win-win. Will some employees occasionally take advantage of your good nature toward their personal lives? Perhaps. Perhaps not. But the trade-off is that overall you will retain a stable of happier employees who will feel more content at work and likely remain loyal employees for the foreseeable future. It's basic respect. And remember that whole "reap what you sow" thing? That.

6

Be a Lock Box

For secrets. For family difficulties. For any communication between you and a team member that you know is meant to be confidential.

In short, be a Lock Box for secrets. This is a sure-fire ingredient toward achieving and strengthening trust in you, Boss.

No one likes drama in the workplace, and very often drama begins with gossip and the sharing of information which was clearly meant to be kept private.

You'll find that the more your employees learn they can trust you with, the more they will trust you with, and you will cultivate a team that believes in *you* as their leader.

7

Say Something Nice/Kind on a Regular Basis

Be sincere. Say something nice, give a compliment, make a kind remark.

Everybody needs an "Atta boy!" from time to time, or at least a pleasant boost to their day. One of the best things you can do on a regular basis to instill harmony and a sense of good, positive morale in your team is to give a sincere compliment whenever possible. And yes, it should always be sincere. Nearly everyone can sense a ruse or flat, feigned flattery.

Simple words can mean a great deal to someone's sense of self-esteem, purpose, and overall climate of the day. Sincere compliments, such as:

"That color looks nice on you."

"Your hair looks really good today."

"I like the way you handled that difficult customer/guest/visitor/applicant."

"Good job on the reports this week."

"New shoes? Nice!"

"You have good posture."

"It's always nice to see you in the office. You make our workplace brighter."

"Your kids look really happy in that picture."

It goes without saying, of course, that the compliments will fall within the realm of acceptable and non-offensive ones, and that in no way could they be construed as harassment. Simple, sincere kindness. Kind words. You will be sowing seeds of pleasantry in your pool of employees that you will harvest over and over again.

8

Communication is Key

When companies perform regular yearly surveys about the organization and its management, it frequently comes to light that the Boss' weakest performance point is in the area of communication. This failure becomes an easy habit because it is the responsibility as well as privilege of the Boss to decide exactly what and what not to communicate to the subordinate team. Many Bosses take a lackadaisical approach to communication, either procrastinating (which often results in little-to-no delivery of relevant information at all), or abbreviating crucial information in such a way that employees end up with a dearth of knowledge that would make their jobs easier and more sensical.

Communication that is relevant to job needs and performance should always, without exception, be swift and thorough. There is a sense of security and job-related assurance when team members believe they are fully informed. Information is one of the essential tools that allows every employee to perform at optimum levels.

It should never happen that a team member is caught unaware or embarrassed because the communication from the Boss has failed.

9

Fun and Friendly Competition

The truth of the matter is, we never really grow up. We may be grown-ups on the outside, with varying degrees of responsibility and wisdom, but that just comes with years on the planet. On the inside is a kid who still thrives on fun and games and cartoon humor. If you have any doubt, tune in to Sunday night television and count how many animated series are targeted at us!

It is vital, in the workplace, to maintain a lighthearted culture wherever it is possible and appropriate. As the Boss, you can search for ways to inject random touches of frivolity and contests or appoint someone else to do so.

It is imperative to remember that fun and games lose their happy diversion when one person is always the winner, so make sure you limit repeat wins to a certain number per year or per period. That keeps the enthusiasm fresh each time a competition or game is introduced.

Keep in mind the sorts of prizes that are meaningful to your employees. Gift cards, tickets to events, movies or shows, travel incentives, family outings, free meals - whether frugal or extravagant, the win is a boost to the morale of the whole team, and you, Boss, the source of the boost, will be appreciated. Because you are demonstrating that you appreciate them.

10

Be Supportive, Encouraging and Honest

The absolute most affirming thing any employee in an organization can say about his/her Boss (you!) is that you are supportive and encouraging. Those two qualities hold a treasure trove of respect and loyalty.

Of course, employees will make mistakes and there will be times correction is necessary, and there will be times when a team member is upset over the correction. But, such exceptions notwithstanding, cultivating an atmosphere of support and encouragement, along with transparency and maintaining a reputation for being honest, will glean you employee longevity and support in return.

Reap what you sow.

What do *support* and *encouragement* look like?

- Making sure each team member has access to all the tools necessary to get the job done
- Whenever possible, redirecting before correcting.
- Ask the employee how a problematic situation could have been handled differently - you're teaching how to solve the problem.
- Be swift to acknowledge the wins, the improvements, and the moments when work has gone above-and-beyond what was needed.
- Be just as swift to admit a mistake on your part - the Boss who knows how to apologize will have a more cohesive and dedicated team.

11

Maintain Clear Expectations

This is an adjunct to point 8, Communication. It is an indispensable matter in your workplace culture. When every employee in your organization has a perspicuous understanding of what is required of them, the work culture and resulting atmosphere will settle, and much of the drama that may have come from job-related confusions will dissipate.

Make sure to communicate clearly, stating and clarifying even what may seem like an obvious point. Ask and answer what may seem like obvious questions - this avoids later confusions and mistakes borne of miscommunication.

Remember that if for any reason those expectations change, it is imperative to make sure all team members are made aware of the changes. Explain, if at all possible, why the changes happened and how it affects the team and/or the company. If, for any reason, you are not in a position to freely explain the reasons behind the changes, make that clear as well. Be honest.

12

Regard Employees as People First, Not Numbers

Ask any Boss what the most challenging part of the job is, and the majority of them will say it's managing the employees. It's often remarked that it sometimes feels like "babysitting."

It is exactly this sort of thought process that breeds more difficulty among the troops.

Remember, earlier - people will rise to the level of your expectations.

Each person is an individual, with a plethora of idiosyncrasies, a lifetime of history, joys, sorrows, and bags of baggage. And so are you. Respect them as such and handle them with respect.

Listening and not disparaging. Advising and not castigating. Correcting and redirecting, whenever possible. And not just in public, but in private, and also to the other team members. Gossip and trash-talking others should be absolutely forbidden in your organization. When you must discuss disciplinary difficulties, do so behind closed doors, and should the occasion arise that you are discussing one team member with another, never allow yourself to disrespect either one.

Set the example.

It certainly is a challenge. But you're up to it, Boss. And you will infect your workplace with an aura of mutual respect and esteem.

13

Reward Any Above-and-Beyond Job Performance

Be swift to acknowledge any successful job-related activity that goes above and beyond what is expected.

Did a team member come in early to help on a project that was not his/her responsibility? Did someone go out of his/her way to do extra market research? When a key employee was out sick, did another spontaneously step in to cover the responsibilities? Did the team leader do a great job re-organizing the workplace without being asked?

There are countless ways an employee may contribute outside of what is expected, and while there are times a sincere word of appreciation will suffice - even make a lasting impression, there are other times a gesture will have more meaningful effect. Especially when the employee didn't perform the task for the purpose of gain, a reward such as a gift card, tickets, or a free lunch will truly communicate that you value not just the task, but also the person who chose to go above-and-beyond for the company.

The Boss who *demonstrates* "Thank you" is a Boss whose team will be both loyal and successful.

14

Make Goals Tangible

In the course of setting objectives for your employees, make sure

- a) It is written down. Give each team member a printed copy of the goals you have set. Have them initial that they received the copy. No one can deny having the information, and you have invested in clear communication.

- b) It is just beyond the last achievement, but still reachable with proper effort and application. If the goal is too lofty it will quickly be regarded as completely unreachable by the very employees who should be leaning toward attaining progress and not away from it.

c) Time frames, if any, are clearly spelled out. Make it so obvious there couldn't possibly be a misunderstanding about the deadlines.

d) Give clear guidelines, if necessary, about how you expect the goals to be achieved, what will increase the likelihood of achieving it, and what may be the positive outcome of reaching the goal. Bonus? Pizza party? Tickets to an event or a game arcade restaurant? Gift cards? Dinner out on the Boss?

15

Review Consistently

While it may be one of the most annoying administrative tasks on the roster, a yearly or semi-annual review is essential to being a good Boss. A review gives you, Boss, the opportunity to clearly and officially convey to each team member his/her personal pros and cons as it relates to job performance and contribution to the company.

Some reviews will be a delight, and others will be less so. It must be done, and it must be done regularly. It is a part of clear communications, and beyond the matter of documenting things, it dusts off all of the notions that bad habits go unnoticed or that good ones go unacknowledged. Without regular reviews there is no compass for correction, and your employees may not stay on course.

16

Host Social Events

At least annually, you need to sponsor a company party, one where family members are welcome and included. A holiday party, a summer BBQ picnic, a fancy catered affair in the box at the stadium - make sure it is an event just enough out of the ordinary that it generates some excitement and good attendance.

To encourage employees to show up to the party, reward each one who attends with an extra paid day (or two!) off in the upcoming year.

Why is this important to your success as a Boss? Because each time you can pull your employees together into a cohesive unit you strengthen the team, and to do so outside of work with no agenda but to enjoy themselves (and include the family!) at a place and in a manner that they probably would not otherwise experience - well, it's a room full of warm fuzzies all over.

And sometimes, to be a great Boss, you just gotta do something nice for them.

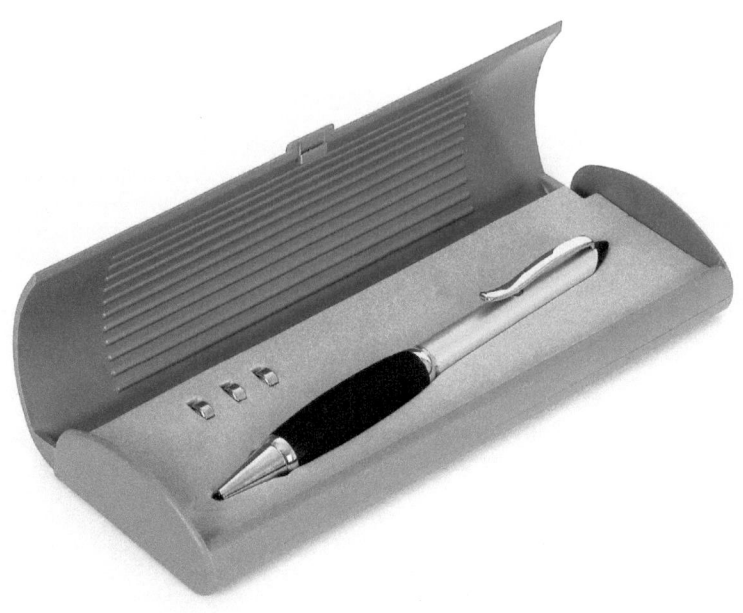

17

Acknowledge Milestones

Milestone anniversaries with the company merit a celebration - a pin, an award, a gift, and a moment of public recognition in front of peers. Just a moment is all it takes, unless the milestone is really remarkable. Five years with the organization merits a different regard than, say, twenty-five.

When you take the time and make the effort to make your employee feel special and appreciated for the time invested in service to your company, you are not only doing the right thing, but also you are demonstrating more than "thank you" can express.

The other team members will look forward to their own moment of recognition. Good job, Boss. You invested in a small moment that will return employee retention.

18

Maintain a Calm Demeanor

Of course there are going to be moments you really feel like a good display of temper is appropriate, whether due to employee shortcomings and mistakes or other business events beyond the scope of the team's responsibility. You will feel a good rage coming on and the urge to rail (or at least raise your voice a good bit) will seem well-deserved.

But, a good Boss doesn't do it.

It is indescribably important to understand that your employees should never, EVER fear you, and the occasional (or frequent) show of temper will result in just exactly that. Regardless of the speed at which you recover your calm, the scar on your staff will be long-lasting. Only tyrants and ancient kings rule through fear.

Solve the problem. Discuss the situation's failings and what you expect from that point forward, and move on.

You will find that when your employees observe your handling even the most infuriating situation with composure and restraint, they will gain a measure of trust in you that you did not expect possible. The kind of trust that pulls them TOWARD you when they need to confess a mistake or ask for help rather than leaning away and dreading the admission. You will be the one they seek for advice and direction.

Many Bosses fail miserably at this point and the disrespect and general disruption to the company culture may become so palpable that the staff actually become an unreliable, unstable team.

No temper tantrums. Ever!

19

Admit Mistakes and Never Hesitate to Apologize

This is another point that falls back on just exactly how to generate respect. Remember, you are setting the example, and being too proud to admit an error isn't going to strengthen your organization. In fact, just the opposite; a haughty Boss who is too proud or stubborn to admit even the most obvious mistake will result in gossip, grumbling, and a general whispering campaign that works to the detriment of the company's effectiveness. It divides a workforce.

If you, the Boss, know how to apologize, each reporting employee will quickly learn the (often difficult) lesson. There is a tremendous peace within an organization when each person - including the Boss - owns up to mistakes in thinking, words, or action.

Many mistakes are innocent. Some are less so. Some are complete blunders. Admit them, smile, and move on with a team who knows they can trust you as the strong Boss leader you are.

20

Be Consistent

Every employee needs to know exactly who you are going to be when he/she shows up for work each day. Mood swings, temperamental demonstrations, metaphorical storms and lashing out are never conducive to a good work atmosphere nor to staff retention.

If you expect each staff member to report to work, leave the personal problems and baggage outside the front door, and to engage and perform the duties assigned each day, then make no doubt about it, they all learn that from watching you.

You are their trusted leader, Boss, and as such, your team needs to know you are exactly the person they expect you to be, day in and day out. It ensures calm and a true sense of camaraderie among the staff when they never have to tremble at the thought of your showing up in a "mood."

Important Conclusion

You may have noticed that some of these points are related, and that nearly all of them circle back to Set the Example. In our modern culture it is a frequent admonition: Be the Change You Want to See.

Yes, you are the Boss, and it can be a complicated environment in which to make changes and implement setting a good example. And, truthfully, there are workplaces where it really does sometimes feel like you are "babysitting," but it is in just such an environment that a strong, trustworthy, example-setting, supportive, encouraging Boss is most valuable.

As stated in the introduction, this is not a book about how to do your job. Obviously you are doing a very good job or you wouldn't be the Boss, right?

This is a handbook - a reference of 20 simple rules to enact. No one needs to know you are putting these guidelines into practice but you. Do so. Use the guidelines, and as you enact them take notice of the changes you see in your direct reports and ultimately the entire team.

As you work these rules into your routine and make them a habit - give it time to really become the customary culture in your organization - you will see weak teams become stronger, strong teams become more productive and cohesive, and a sense of calm settle into the workplace.

You are deserving of a strong workforce. You have the ability to cultivate and draw out the very best in each member of your teams. You can. Pay attention. Enact these guidelines.

Be a Better Boss!

www.ingramcontent.com/pod-product-compliance
Lightning Source LLC
Chambersburg PA
CBHW040328220526

45473CB00009B/2609